Oedipus The Vi

David Greig was born in Edinburgh. His p
The American Pilot, *Europe*, *The Architec* ...ui, *The*
Cosmonaut's Last Message, *Victoria*, *Outlying Islands* and *San Diego*. His work with Suspect Culture includes: *One Way Street*, *Airport*, *Timeless*, *Mainstream*, *Casanova* and *8000M*. David's translation of *Caligula* was presented at the Donmar Warehouse in an award winning production in 2003. His work for children and young people includes: *Danny 306*, *Me Forever* and *Dr Korczak's Example*.

Capercaillie Books

Oedipus The Visionary

by David Greig

Capercaillie Books

CAPERCAILLIE BOOKS LIMITED

This version of *Oedipus* first published by Capercaillie Books Limited in 2005.

Registered Office 1 Rutland Court, Edinburgh.

© 2005 David Greig. The moral right of the author has been asserted.

Design by Ian Kirkwood Design.

Typeset by Chimera Creations in Cosmos and Veljovic.

Printed in Great Britain by Antony Rowe Ltd., Chippenham, Wiltshire.

A catalogue record for this book is available from the British Library.

ISBN 0-9549625-1-6.

The publisher acknowledges support from the Scottish Arts Council towards the publication of this title.

For Tom McGrath

Introduction

I remember the first time I encountered the story of Oedipus. I must have been about eight years old and I was sitting at the corner of the big family dining room table in our bungalow in Jos, Nigeria. In front of me was a paperback book folded open. The book must have been some compendium of world mythology, which my mother would have bought from Chanrai's, the Asian run department store in town. Mr Chanrai stocked an eccentric selection of children's books but my mother pretty much bought them all – on the basis I suppose that any book is better than none. I remember obtaining with some excitement Geoffrey Trease's history of Norse Mythology at the same period. It was a thick paperback with a rather exciting line drawing of Ygdrasil, the tree of life, on its purple cover. I don't know on what basis Chanrai chose his stock. I don't suppose there was an immense demand for the stories of Valhalla in provincial Northern Nigeria in the 1970's. Nor, for that matter, was there a thirst for the myths of Greece and Rome. I wonder if Mr Chanrai just happened by a schools supplier with a job lot of mythology books? However it came about, since there wasn't really any television available to me, Mr Chanrai's eccentric children's book selection pretty much defined my early outlook on the world.

If my memory of the circumstances is vague, my memory of the sensation the story of *Oedipus* induced in me is still powerful and precise. Bright warm sunlight is streaming in through the dining room window. Victor, the cook, is preparing shepherd's pie for my tea in the kitchen. I close the book, and I feel a little sick and I have a very profound sense of injustice. 'That can't be right.' I think. 'Is that the end of the story? Could the gods be so unfair? Could the world be so unfair? Could life be so unfair?' As I replayed the events of the story, letting them settle in my mind, I was overcome with a mixture of fear, horror, and pleasure. It was my first taste of that nauseating fascination that comes of hearing about an awful fate that has befallen someone other than oneself. It was my first taste of catharsis.

   Oedipus does seem, in retrospect, rather a salty book for a small boy. By Freudian standards I probably wasn't that long past my own Oedipal family drama at the time. Perhaps this is why it affected me so strongly, although I doubt it. I felt the same pity and terror at the blank, brutal, indifference of the universe the first time I read Mr Bump – another Chanrai gem – and Mr Bump didn't kill his father or sleep with his mother: he was simply Bump by name and bump by nature. No, I don't think *Oedipus* spoke to me because of the dark internal desires it supposedly describes. I prefer to take the story at face value. *Oedipus* speaks to us because it is a story about the possibility, the terrifying possibility that we must keep buried for the sake of our sanity, that all the suffering and horror in the world really is our fault. I think *Oedipus* speaks to us because is a story about guilt.

   When Theatre Babel approached me in 1998 with the idea of adapting Sophocles *Oedipus The King*, I was very clear that I didn't want to do a translation. Apart from the fact that there are many fine translations in existence already, I didn't feel artistically inspired by the idea of literary authenticity. I was far more interested in emotional authenticity. I wanted to find a world in which I could re-tell Sophocles' story so that it would feel to a modern audience just as shocking, violent and nihilistic as if it were one of the so called 'In Yer Face' plays which were dominating the British theatre at that time. I didn't want the audience to watch with their fingers stroking their chins, pondering the fineness of the poetry. I wanted them to reel back in their seats. I wanted to re-capture that first feeling I had on reading *Oedipus* as a child: the pity and terror, the catharsis.

   In 1999 I visited my brother, Michael, who was setting up a

nature reserve in the Meluti Mountains of Lesotho. Lesotho is a poor, rural country completely surrounded by South Africa. The Meluti hills are ten thousand feet high – enough to induce dizziness and headaches in lowland visitors. The people of the area live in the many small villages and hamlets dotted over the hill tops and perched on the steep slopes above terraced fields. There are very few roads, most people move around on foot, or on horseback. The people live mostly from subsistence farming and livestock grazing. One road leads through and out of the mountains into South Africa. Along this road, huff and puff the overworked taxi buses, taking young men to work in the far away mines and factories of Johannesburg. It is the remittances from these economic migrants that keep the area alive.

My brother's job involved him working very closely with local communities as well as and leading a team of Lesothans who would eventually take over the running of the national park from him. While I was there, he was kind enough to take me with him to meet and talk to many of the people he worked with. It was, for me, a fascinating and surprising glimpse into the world of rural Africa.

The Basuto people are a sophisticated, independent people, and fully aware of modern technology and global economics. However, the combination of rural poverty and limited educational opportunities has meant that, in the villages modernity coexists with the social structures and beliefs which remain largely as they have been for centuries. Like the rest of Southern Africa, Lesotho has also been ravaged by AIDS. In the absence of affordable retro-viral drugs to treat the illness it's easy for fear and taboo to take hold. Many people seek treatment from the local Mnagka or Shaman. The Mnagka is able to communicate across the real world and the spirit world. Someone suffering from an illness may be identified as a being a victim of bad 'muti'. Muti is a multilayered word, which means medicine and luck, power and magic. It describes a force in the world which, although invisible and spiritual, is a real and powerful as electricity. It's important to remember that plague – everywhere and at every time throughout history – draws people towards supernatural explanations. It is not only the rural Basuto who seek meanings for AIDS from the spirit world. While I was in South Africa I heard one Afrikaner woman openly saying that she believed the disease was a punishment sent by God.

The presence both of plague and the supernatural in the ordinary lives of people seemed to me to present a suitably contemporary world in which to set a new version of *Oedipus*. But I was clear that I didn't want to make exact, pedantic parallels between the Greek theology, which backed up *Oedipus Rex*, and contemporary Africa. For me the process was more fluid. The experiences I had in Lesotho grounded the poetry of *Oedipus* in a contemporary reality but the play is still set in Thebes. It's simply that Thebes is imagined in a new way – a combination of past and present, old and new.

The other driving force of my reimagining was an engagement with power and economics. While I was in South Africa my brother and I travelled around the country and I came to realise that every pretty, prosperous seeming little town with its watered green lawns was paired with a ramshackle, black township serviced by standpipes and without electricity. Next to the town of Furiesburg is the township of Mashaeng; next to Johannesburg is Soweto. The people of the township, invariably black, work in the low paid menial, agricultural and domestic jobs that sustain the prosperity of the nearby 'white' town. This grotesque geography is a legacy of apartheid. And yet, while it is shocking to see this inequality so close up, it seems important to ask whether prosperous Edinburgh, or Stirling or Milngavie have their townships too? Maybe not a township in a single geographical location but a 'virtual' township, an amalgamation of many different places and people: the housing estates where the omnipresence of long-

4

term unemployment keeps the wages of unskilled workers down. The agricultural poly tunnels and pack houses of Andalusia where illegal migrant labour from North Africa supply Tesco's and Sainsbury's with fresh vegetables throughout the winter. Or, further afield, the anonymous sweatshops in the industrial zones of southern China where our clothes are made and our electronic good fabricated. Perhaps, if our township existed as blatantly as it does in South Africa we would find it intolerable. But, like so much else in Scotland, the architecture of power is rather elegantly executed and so the ugly realities are kept out of sight.

I am distanced from the effects of my power. I buy a cup of coffee and don't need to know about the living conditions of the people who grow the beans. I eat meat but never have to see how the animals I eat are kept and killed. I enjoy the convenience of a mobile phone without ever having to confront the violence and rape caused by the four armies in the Congo fighting over the mineral rights to mine tantalum which makes my phone work. And yet – I am not inhuman. When I do chance to glimpse at the poverty and misery that afflicts so many people in the world I recoil in horror. I look at an awful famine or plague in some African dictatorship and I shout at the screen – 'who is responsible for this? I demand answers.' – without realising that if I insist on digging for an answer I may discover that the person responsible is me.

I never felt that telling the story of *Oedipus* was an easy process. I never found it smooth. *Oedipus Rex* is an eternal mountain within the landscape of western literature – it existed before me and will long outlive me. Writing my own version, I felt like a climber negotiating its dark slopes of scree and cliff in the mist. Sometimes the journey required each foot to be placed forward carefully and patiently; one step at a time. In other sections I could only strike out boldly into the unknown and hope I didn't fall. In the end, I believe this book, *Oedipus The Visionary*, to represent simply one route up that old mountain. It is a new route and, I hope it will prove an enduring one, but nonetheless it can only ever be one way of approaching a myth and a play which form the very definition of the western mind.

David Greig, 2005

Characters

OEDIPUS: a landowner.

JOCASTA: his wife.

CREON: Jocasta's brother and farm manager.

KING: the highest ranked man in the township.

PRIEST: a local priest.

TIRESIAS: an educated man from a family of seers.

MESSENGER: a foreign domestic servant in fifties.

HERDBOY: old man.

SERVANT: domestic servant.

OEDIPUS' CHILDREN

GUARDS

CHORUS

Setting

The Thebes imagined in this play is a place which perhaps most closely resembles the Matibo Drakenseberg mountains of South Africa at some point in the late twentieth century. This information is offered as inspiraion and should not be considered a limitation in the interpretation of the play in performance.

Note on the Chorus

The Chorus represent different elements of society at different times. Sometimes they are villagers, sometimes a mob, sometimes the rich, sometimes the poor. At certain points they are individuated as 'Man 1' or 'Woman 1'. This individuation should be respected. Apart from this, the manner of choric speech and any addition of music or movement are left entirely to the discretion of the producer.

Scene 1

Late evening. A tree fallen beside a dry riverbed. A dying man lies semi conscious on the ground. The CHORUS enter, slowly, watching him. He tries to crawl away. Fails.

CHORUS: He wants water,
    There's none.
    He's licking at the dust.
    Do you know him?
    Never seen him,
    He's sniffing the ground, he thinks he can smell a river.
    There's no river there.
    There used to be a river.
    Not now.
    A cruel river trick that: to leave its smell behind.
    Is he dead?
    No.
    He's hanging on.
    Give him a kick. See if he moves.
    We might as well sit.
    It's too hot to stand.
    Vultures 'll come soon.

The CHORUS sit. Silence. After a painful amount of time.

MAN: Kill me.
    Please.

No one moves. He slumps.

CHORUS: I think we should say a prayer.
    Let us pray.
    Dear God.
    Please dear God.
    Immortal God.
    God of pain.
    God of the sea.
    God of the earth.
    God of grief.
    It seems we still have some pity left.
    Disease has destroyed us.
    We're parched.
    Starving.
    Penniless.
    Powerless.
    Homeless.
    Restless
    and emptied of hope.
    But it seems we still have pity in us.
    A damp stain on the dust where a lake once was.
    We beg you god.
    Send armies of flaming angels.
    Send lightning.
    Send a hail of bullets into our hearts
    and kill the pity in us.
    Dear fat god.
    Dear drunken god.
    God on your throne of battered gold leaf.
    In your rooms of red velvet.
    With your naked, laughing whores sat on your lap.
    Your mouth stained red with wine.
    Make us like you.
    Give us the power of your hate.

The power of a God to see pain and feel nothing.
Hear our prayer.
Wound our souls with fire.
Give us strength.
Plunge our hearts in the fire of divine hate.
Cauterize our souls against this fatal human feeling – pity.

He's dead now.

Scene 2

Bright sunlight. A lush garden. A swimming pool. Nearby, a razor wire fence patrolled by two armed, uniformed GUARDS. Behind the wire, dust and the CHORUS.

JOCASTA sits in a deckchair. In a swimming costume, wet from the pool. OEDIPUS enters, wearing workclothes, dusty and tired.

OEDIPUS: Sometimes I wish the sun would never rise again.
    The world's reversed.
    Our fertile land's turned killer.
    Night's kinder on the eyes than day.
    I don't want to look at any more starving people.
    I don't want to look at their pitiful children.
    Or see their bodies falling apart.
    Or smell the shit and death stink from their village.
    Or witness another subhuman wretch steal meat from off the bones of a burnt corpse.
    This is become a cruel place now.
    Do you want a beer?

JOCASTA: Get the boy to bring one.
    Sit down. You're worried. Sit beside me.

    Bring Master two beers!
    Cool your feet.

She helps him take off his boots. He places his feet in the pool water.

JOCASTA: A kiss for poor queen.

They kiss.

OEDIPUS: You taste clean.

JOCASTA: Of course.

OEDIPUS: Let me look at you.
    Beautiful.
    What a relief.
    Your fertile body,
    after so much barren land.
    You're warm and wet
    after a day of dust
    you give me life again.

A SERVANT arrives with a tray, two beers and two glasses. JOCASTA pours. She lies dose to him.

JOCASTA: It's sad.
    I used to love this time of year.
    When I was a child.
    All you could see were fields and fields of tall grass.
    And orange groves.
    I used to walk through the orange groves on the first day of summer. All the families had come for the harvest and there was me with my little white parasol and my little dog beside me barking, barking at the men. And they made such a terrible fuss of me then. smiling and laughing. They would lift a ladder against a tree and say 'Jocasta, madam please'. And I'd climb

the rough ladder, up I'd go and at the top I'd reach up and the fruit would be so heavy I'd only touch it and it'd drop into my hands. I would balance on top of the ladder and dig my thumb into the pith to open the orange and, you know, I could see the fields and the fat cattle and our land seemed to stretch all the way to the mountains. And the ladder shook and the dust rose from the feet of the dancing women beating the ground. Then the smell of orange spray and the taste of the year's first mouthful of fruit. Around me a blur of groves and fruit and grass and cattle and birds, birds in the deep sky wheeling slowly slowly waiting to drop down and kill some ground animal.

And in winter. Only white snow,

Brilliant white.

Maddeningly white snow and a black road winding. My father walking down the black road through the snow with his gun slung over his shoulder looking for vermin . . .

It was nice. It was a bloody nice time then.

OEDIPUS: Maybe, we should go somewhere . . . Europe.

Get away from this hell.

Take the kids and . . . the two of us.

Let the land die behind us

And start again.

JOCASTA: Drink. You'll fix things. You should be confident and strong. You weaken yourself by grieving for people who're already lost.

This is your land now.

Rule it.

Make it like it was before,

oranges and snow and deep sky.

And then, then when next summer comes.

We'll have fun. We'll drive through the desert hunting deer.

I'll stand on the roof and hold the searchlight.

I'll slice open the night.

And catch eyes of dazzled animals illuminated, still.
As though the ground is embedded with stars.
And you'll raise the rifle and shoot straight and clear.
We'll have fun.
Won't we, next summer?

OEDIPUS: I promise.

Scene 3

A low table set with small bowls of nuts. Two glasses and two beers. OEDIPUS and the KING sit on low stools. The KING wears a short sleeved nylon shirt outside grey, stained suit trousers. The PRIEST stands nearby. He wears a stained but clean t-shirt with an advertising slogan on it. His trousers are ragged but clean. Behind the razor wire, still patrolled by the GUARDS, stand the CHORUS.

OEDIPUS: The country's covered with the ash of funeral fires. The wind that blows in from the sea picks up the dust of corpses and blows black clouds towards the mountain. Even the rain's black. My swimming pool carries a skin of black dust. My wife can't sleep for the cries of women carried up from the township on the night air. Your grief reminds us of our happiness. Your dead children remind us that ours still breathe . . .

I know you think you can't come to me.

In normal times there's a barrier between us – dogs and wire. But these are not normal times.

Your people are my responsibility, just as if they were my children.

You know who I am, you call me Oedipus.

Everyone in the district knows me.

So I'm not afraid of you.

I want to hear the truth for myself.
I know you'll speak honestly.
You're the older man.
Tell me.
What are the people saying?

KING: Oedipus. You're a strong man. You're not cruel and we
know you can see clearly enough. Everyone has gathered in
the shadow of your farm. Men and women. The boys who're
too young to take cattle to the mountains, the old people
burdened by life's cruel sights, the priests who perform our
ceremonies. Even the young men and women who're the
future of our people.
Everyone has come looking for your protection.
The priests have built altars in the dust of the riverbeds,
they've consulted the stars, and interpreted the movements of
animals but death is all they can see sir.
Death in the sky.
Death in the sea.
Death in our cattle.
Death in the crops.
Death invades the pregnant stomach.
Death spits fever over the faces of our infants.
Death beats on our doors.
Death bathes in our blood.
Death arouses himself with our grief.
Death becomes drunk on our misery.
So we turn to you.
Perhaps you're not a god but you're the most powerful man
we know. You built the dam which saved us from the drought.
You built that road that brought us trade. You drove away the
stockthieves who bankrupted us with cattle theft.
You have knowledge and there are those among us who say
you must have the protection of a god.
I must say I believe them.

15

You rule this land.
But unless you act you'll be owner of a wilderness.
Consult with your god.
Act on his advice.
This is what people are saying.

OEDIPUS: I have no god.
No protection from any god.
God didn't build the dam, or road or drive away your persecutors it was a man, men. A person. Me.
If there's a reason for this plague.
I will find and cure it.
No business of god.

KING: As you wish.

OEDIPUS: I sent my brother in law, Creon, to the city to consult the oracle. He's supposed to have come back. He isn't here.

KING: Do you think these men can save us?

OEDIPUS: I don't know. When Creon returns I'll send for you.

KING: . . .

OEDIPUS pours a beer.

OEDIPUS: Please, have some more.

KING: No.

OEDIPUS: As soon as Creon's back I'll send a messenger. Now I have to work.

KING: The people are suffering terribly.

OEDIPUS: I'm working in order to find a —

KING: I'm asking you to respect —

OEDIPUS: No. Let me tell you this. Any pain you people feel is as nothing to my pain in watching them suffer.

I'm in pain too.
I can't sleep I want to run, to escape to some healthy place but –
Creon should be here now.
Don't ask me to display my feelings.
It only blurs clear vision.

KING: I must ask you not to speak to me in this way.

OEDIPUS: Why?

KING: Because I am a King.
And these are my people.
If you raise your voice to me you insult me.
And if you insult me, you insult them.

OEDIPUS: I'm sorry. I didn't realise .
I'm still a foreigner here.

KING: I must not be sent away.
Or sent for.

OEDIPUS: Of course.
You must do as is –
Whatever you want.
Ask.

KING: The people ask that you perform a ritual.

OEDIPUS: You understand I don't share your beliefs.

KING: We have no beliefs.

OEDIPUS: I put my faith in truth alone.

KING: As we do.

OEDIPUS: Is there a priest here.

KING: This man is my priest.

OEDIPUS: What's the purpose of the ritual.

KING: It's the ritual we perform in situations such as this. It has no other purpose.

OEDIPUS: The people want me to –
 Do I have to take part?

KING: No.

OEDIPUS: Only watch?

KING: It's only necessary that you be present.

OEDIPUS: Then perform the ritual.

The KING approaches the priest, whispers in his ear.

KING: He says he can perform it here.

The PRIEST takes some materials from a bag including some newspaper. He clears some space. He places the newspaper in the space.

PRIEST: Water.

OEDIPUS gives him a beer. He takes a swig of the beer and then he walks in a circle around the newspaper pouring the beer to define the circle. He crouches. He sets fire to the paper. It burns. When the burning is finished he remains still. Looking at the ashes.

OEDIPUS: What do the ashes say?

PRIEST: I don't understand.

OEDIPUS: What do you see?

PRIEST: I see ashes.

OEDIPUS: I see ashes.

PRIEST: Yes.

OEDIPUS: But is there – you're a priest – any interpretation . . .

Is there something else?

PRIEST: Yes sir

OEDIPUS: What? Answers? A cure.

PRIEST: Ashes.

OEDIPUS: Only ashes. Surely the ashes tell you something.

PRIEST: That there was a fire here.

OEDIPUS: King, I'll need the help of more than priests to drive away plague. This man sees only what's in front of his face.

KING: It's considered a great gift sir, to see so clearly.

Scene 4

Night. A bright porch light from OEDIPUS' house illuminates the garden. In the background, behind the wire, many fires. CREON arrives. His suit is dishevelled, his shirt hanging out. He has a wound to his head.

CREON: Good news.
　　It's fine. All fine.

OEDIPUS: Where have you been.

CREON: It's OK The whole thing's fine.

OEDIPUS: What happened?

CREON: Car broke.

OEDIPUS: How?

CREON: Fuck knows. Honestly, It's beyond me.

OEDIPUS: Did you talk to the oracle.

CREON: It's fine. It all makes sense.

OEDIPUS: What did they tell you?

CREON: Shh.

OEDIPUS: Tell me.

CREON: Lets not panic. Lets not . . . shhh.
  Who's listening?
  Darkness brother, shh, stars, fires, ears.
  Children's ears to hear.
  Then they run down to the township and tell.

OEDIPUS: I don't care who hears.

CREON searches his pockets. Earth falls out of his trouser pockets. He discovers another injury on his leg. Eventually he finds a crumpled piece of paper.

OEDIPUS: What happened to you?

CREON: Jumped. Bastards. Fucking little cunts jumped me.
  I'm taking a piss by the side of the road.
  Under the twinkling stars.
  Whistling along to the radio.
  And the cunts rise up out the long grass to rob me.
  I saw them off.
  Shot each and every one of the little fuckers through the head.
  Still.
  Needed a drink after that.
  Needed a fuck after the drink.
  That's why I took so long.

OEDIPUS: This is the report?

CREON: Shh. OK, OK here. (**CREON reads from piece of paper.**)
  'Unpollute the air you breathe.
  Uncorrupt the rotten earth.
  Every household and every life is touched by crime.

No reconciliation is possible with this crime, no redemption.
Only purification through blood and violence can wash this
land clean'.

OEDIPUS: What crime?

CREON: Murder. Apparently.

OEDIPUS: Whose murder?

CREON: Laius. One of us.
Before your time.

OEDIPUS: I've heard of him.

CREON: We've to find out who killed him and bring them to justice.

OEDIPUS: Where do they want us to look?

CREON: Fuck knows.
Read it yourself.
I'm going to bed. My skull's thumping.

OEDIPUS: The boy'll see to your wounds.
Tomorrow we can begin the investigation.

CREON: I wouldn't bother. It's finished out here. Give it up brother.

OEDIPUS: Never.
This is the key.
We can solve this now.
We have to, don't you see, not for their sake, but for ours as
well. If they killed one of us. Already they attacked you, who
next. The plague's attacking the whole township, they're close
to anarchy. How long can our house stay safe?

CREON: Listen sunshine boy.
My family took this land three hundred years ago with four
guns and a bible.
We held it for generations against these savages.
With our fingertips we scraped the earth till it gave us crops.

Crops fertilised by this family's sweat and blood.
And still.
We're sent plague, anarchy, drought and revolution.
Well fuck it.
Fuck the god of nature that damns us.
I'm sick of struggle.
I'm going to live in the city.
Too many stars in this damn place twinkling like cunts who enjoy watching me suffer.
Lonely.
There's more of us in the city and streetlights instead of stars.
The land itself hates us.
I'm going.
One day I'm going and I'll never come back.

Scene 5

Daylight. A patch of dusty earth. Some kind of market place. Each member of the CHORUS lays out a ragged cloth and places on it a selection of worthless random objects. This is a market in which people sell the little they still possess.

MAN 1: I'm saving up to go to college.
   To the Harvard school of business.

MAN 2: I'm sick of living every day on dry bread and boiled cabbage stalks. I'm going to buy a fucking happy meal.

WOMAN 1: My daughters are sick.
   With the money I get I'm going to travel to the capital.
   I'm going to buy an air ticket to somewhere very far away.

MAN 1: I'll study hard. And live on nothing.

I'll be the best in my class.

WOMAN 1: I won't travel to the capital in a taxi, or a tram or even a bus.
I can't afford to.

MAN 2: I want to feel the warm burger meat fill my stomach.
Drink the cold drink.
Sit on the red chair.
And know that I have done what I wanted, only once.

WOMAN 1: I will walk to the capital. I need every penny for the drugs, which will save my childrens' lives.

MAN 3: I need to pay a debt.

MAN 1: And when I graduate from Harvard,
I'll take a job with a large corporation.
And the corporation will keep me.

WOMAN 1: I've got a piece of paper and on it, written down, the name of the drugs I want.
I'll find a pharmacist.
And buy the drugs for my children.
Then walk back here over the new road.

MAN 3: If I don't pay.
The man I owe will scar my wife's face.

MAN 1: I'll have a big house in some European city.

MAN 3 If I still don't pay.
He'll break my legs.

WOMAN 2: I will listen to jazz music.
I will attend the theatre.

MAN 3: Once the debt is paid.
I'll be able to steep easily.

MAN 4: I am going to pay to fuck a healthy woman.

Once only.

MAN 2: I have known what it's like to shit burger meat onto the dry earth by the roadside.

WOMAN 2: I will to go to the cinema to watch a romantic comedy.

MAN 5: I'm going to use the money to buy a suit.
With the suit I will impress gullible people.
I'll tell them if they give me some small sum,
I can give them information which will make them rich.
Then when they give me money.
I'll tell them to buy a suit

MAN 4: I'm going to put the cash on a horse.

MAN 6: I'll only buy drink with it
Then I'll go to a place I know.
A dark valley, not far from here.
The grass there is still lush.
I will lie under a tree, alone.
And I'll drink.
And when I'm drunk.
I'll drink more.
And when I'm very drunk.
I'll drink more,
And then I'll ask myself what my name is.
And if I can remember it.
I'll drink more.
And when I'm no longer conscious of anything.
I'll smash one of the bottles on a rock.
And cut my throat with the glass.

Scene 6

The township. Day. OEDIPUS enters. The KING walks with him. OEDIPUS has two GUARDS with him. Crowds gather round him, the crowd is curious but suspicious. They are kept at a little distance from him. A woman comes forward. OEDIPUS draws back.

OEDIPUS: What does she want?

KING: She wants you to touch her.

OEDIPUS: Why?

KING: She wants a blessing. She's dying.

GUARDS push the woman back.

OEDIPUS: Stop. Wait. Leave her.

The GUARDS leave the woman.

OEDIPUS: I can't give you a blessing.
    I've no power to cure you.
    I have no access to gods.

KING: Go home woman. He refuses your blessing . . .
    Go Take your death away from us.
    You are refused.
    The woman leaves,

OEDIPUS speaks to the GUARDS.

OEDIPUS: Give her food. Personally. From my house.

The KING speaks to the GUARDS.

KING: She's dying. Give the food to the young men.

OEDIPUS: Should I speak to them now?

KING: They're waiting.

OEDIPUS: Just here. Shall I speak here.

KING: Speak here.

OEDIPUS: Do you want to make any kind of introduction?

KING: They know who you are.
    You are Oedipus.

OEDIPUS: I'll just speak now then,

KING: Speak now.

The KING gestures, people sit.

OEDIPUS: You've been making offerings to your gods, consulting
    prophets and offering sacrifices to discover the source of the
    plague. Well these prayers have been answered. Do as I tell
    you and the plague will lift and we can all return to peace.
    I, personally, never met this man Laius.
    Nor do I know about his murder.
    But all crime discovers itself in the end, however long it
    remains buried. No guilt can remain in secret forever. Justice
    is always done. This is a law of nature.
    So.
    Listen to me carefully.
    One of you knows who killed Laius.
    Speak.
    I order you.
    You needn't be afraid. A safe exile and the whip of your own
    conscience will be punishment enough.

Silence.

    If one of you knows who the man is.
    Or if the crime was borne of some grudge, some religious

26

reason, even an accident, even if murder was not intended.

I'm asking you to come forward with the truth.

If you have knowledge I will pay a large reward and you will have my eternal gratitude.

Silence.

So, nothing.

Perhaps I should be clear in case there's any doubt.

Someone knows.

My power here is absolute.

I can, and would, kill all of you, if I thought it would unpollute my land.

I will find out.

I will discover the criminal.

Silence.

The killer tells me nothing.

So I'll give him nothing as a reward.

I give him non-existence.

And if it seems to me that anyone has been protecting themselves or others with this silence I now condemn them also to nothingness. I condemn them to live amongst you while their families and the families of their families are cleared from the land, banished and sent over the sea. I will pass a law such that anyone who speaks, or gives shelter, or casts a glance at, or mentions this nothing in their prayers will be killed.

Silence.

Clean up this filthy township.

Whip five of them randomly.

Perhaps chance will see we get the killer.

I order it.

Your silence threatens my country.

I came here, I live and farm this land.
It's mine as if it were the land that bore me.
Better even since home is now as distant in my memory as
it is in miles.
I will fight for this land until my last breath.
How can you sit, in silence and watch it die.
Have you no dignity?
(Pause)
Clean it up.
Clean up your shit and corpses and burn them all.
Empty the water from the dam.
Tear down the shacks that spread stink downwind.
Send the sick to the mountains to die.
Burn what remains of the crops and the cattle.
Talk.
I'm human too.
I'm not a god.
I want to help you.

Silence.

You condemn yourselves with this silence.
I hope you all die.
I hope you all die a dry death under the vultures.
I hope your corpses are stripped by rats.
You deserve plague.
The plague is you.
Reply. Speak. Answer me.

Silence.

KING: I'm standing under this hail of angry words sir.
Looking for some shelter.
If you call down curses you should name those on whom the
curse will fall.

OEDIPUS: Quite right

Did you do it?

KING: No.

OEDIPUS: Why should I believe you.
Why shouldn't I kill you just in case?

KING: People can't tell the truth unless they know it.
Do you want lies?

OEDIPUS: No.

KING: May I suggest . . .

OEDIPUS: Suggest away.
I welcome it.

KING: We have a young man amongst us. Tiresias.
He's been to Europe and studied.
He's also one of our prophets.
When we need knowledge about things beyond our own experience we ask Tiresias.
He has been educated.

OEDIPUS: Send for him.

KING: I've already done so.

OEDIPUS: Good. Fine.

KING: Because, you know. he might be able to cast light on these rumours.

OEDIPUS: What rumours?

KING: Oh sir, not important sir, your search clearly is more efficient but certain people say Laius was killed by one of your people.

OEDIPUS: Who says it?

KING: You know sir. Most probably the ignorant. People who bear grudges, as you say sir, savages.

OEDIPUS: One of my people?

KING: Tiresias can help put an end to these rumours.

OEDIPUS: Send him to my house.
Order these people to clean up the township and tear down
these death infected shacks immediately.

OEDIPUS leaves.

Scene 7

**Evening. The garden. TIRESIAS and OEDIPUS. TIRESIAS is
wearing sunglasses, a clean red T-shirt and blue jeans.
TIRESIAS is blind.**

OEDIPUS: You're Tiresias?

TIRESIAS: Yes.

OEDIPUS: They tell me you're educated.

TIRESIAS: I've been to Europe.

OEDIPUS: Good. So you understand things.
You've got knowledge of the wider world.
A clear vision.
You grasp the nature of plagues.
I've been told to find Laius' killers.
So help me.
You know this place.
You know its history.
You know Its people.
Who do you think's guilty?

TIRESIAS: You don't want to know.
You sent for me and you're asking me questions the answers

to which you don't want to know.
I don't even know why I came.
Maybe I was curious to meet Oedipus.

OEDIPUS: Why don't you sit down. Have a beer with me.

OEDIPUS helps TIRESIAS to a seat. TIRESIAS sits. OEDIPUS gives him a beer. TIRESIAS rejects the offer.

OEDIPUS: Look. I'm aware that normally there is an inhibition between me and the men who work for me. But with you it's different.
You can see things they can't. You're . . . we share an understanding. You can talk freely with me. I'm only interested in truth.

TIRESIAS: I think if we have a beer, maybe discuss literature or something, and then I'll go home.
Pursue the truth if you must.
Discover what you will.
Let me carry the weight of my knowledge alone.

OEDIPUS: This may be hard for you to believe but I promise you. When it comes to the difference between your origins and mine I'm blind. I see an educated man who can help.
That's all.
In fact, I'm glad you're here because I get tired of the ritual the ceremony that I have to go through talking to your people. To deal with phantoms and ghosts all the time. To find a language that rises above the differences between us. Talking to you is like taking a handful of water from a clear stream. It's refreshing.

TIRESIAS: The smell of burning flesh reaches you here I notice.

OEDIPUS: Yes.

TIRESIAS: Still, you have the view, which must be a comfort.
You chose a good place to build the house.

OEDIPUS: It's the obvious choice, if you take into account the lie of the land.
And I planted trees, of course, to shield the house from the wind. and to give shade so . . .
It's good.

TIRESIAS: Can I hear a swimming pool?

OEDIPUS: Yes. Would you like to swim?

TIRESIAS: I can't swim.

OEDIPUS: I can teach you.

TIRESIAS: Describe the scene for me. Please.

OEDIPUS: Of course.
What do you want?

TIRESIAS: Just what you see.

OEDIPUS: The garden, the pool, the dam below us, the cornfields and then, in the middle distance the orange groves and the road. Towards the horizon the hills, Mount Cithairon.

TIRESIAS: What colour is the light over the Cithairon?

OEDIPUS: Grey blue I suppose.

TIRESIAS: To sit with a beer in a place like this.
With a view like this.
Who would think it possible of someone like me.
Yet here I am.
Anything's possible given time and chance.
Isn't that so?

OEDIPUS: Time and chance and the will to make things happen.
It's something we should do more often.
We could work together.

TIRESIAS: No.
It's better if we don't.

OEDIPUS: I don't see why .
We're both men of a new generation.
You and I.
And you could help me save your people.
In fact don't you think it's your duty?
Because you and I are privileged by intelligence and vision.
It's our responsibility to share that.

TIRESIAS: How can you help?
How has anything you've said or done so far helped anyone?
Personally, I'd rather keep my advice to myself if it's no help
to anyone.

OEDIPUS: No help yet, but I'm looking. I've begun the search.
I'm asking you Tiresias, man to man, talk to me.
Tell me the way you see the situation.

TIRESIAS: You really have no idea do you?
I'm telling you I can't talk to you.
Anymore than you can talk to me.

OEDIPUS: So you'ld rather see people dying?

TIRESIAS: Not me. I've killed nobody.

OEDIPUS: You're serious.
You won't help?

TIRESIAS: I won't help you.
You're beyond help.

OEDIPUS: You're a stubborn little bastard aren't you?
You try my patience.
I talk. I open up. I offer – equality here and you.
Sit there like a cold rock.
Superior as though –
A little bit self righteous, a little bit holier than thou.
Have a look at yourself.

TIRESIAS: You try to insult me but you're completely unaware of

33

how ludicrous it sounds to me − hearing these words coming
from your mouth. I'm hearing you describe yourself.

OEDIPUS: You'ld try anyone's patience.
This attitude.
This selfishness when the reality is − your own country's being
devastated.

TIRESIAS: The truth is still there to be found.
Even if I choose not to reveal it.

OEDIPUS: Don't play with fucking language.
I hate that.
What university did you go to exactly?
I can always force the truth out of you.

TIRESIAS: Threaten me with what you like.
I can't talk to you.

OEDIPUS: I will threaten. I'm not sure you understand me.
I believe in no forgiving god. I believe in the god of cause and
effect. If your silence causes more death then I tell you it
would not be a crime in my eyes to scrape the skin from your
body and roll the wounds in petrol until you tell me what I
need to know.
Because you − here − smirking behind your blind eyes.
The feeling I get here is that you've got something to do with
this disaster.
You planned it.
You have the knowledge.
Why? I don't know . . .

TIRESIAS: Finally you're showing yourself.
That's good.
So, Oedipus, you know why we call you Oedipus don't you?

OEDIPUS: Of course.
The name comes from my wounds.
The wounds in my leg that gave this limp.

It means the man who walks with a limp.

TIRESIAS: That's what they tell you.
    But the name also means visionary.

OEDIPUS: It's a good name.

TIRESIAS: The name is given to you ironically.
    Because in seeing so much.
    You see nothing.
    It's a name we use to laugh at you.

OEDIPUS: I don't believe you.

TIRESIAS: So, visionary, you really want to know.
    Who's responsible for the plague.
    I heard you demanding, bullying, threatening in the marketplace.
    Whoever knows and keeps silent about their guilt, let them die under the vultures.
    Well, what plagues my people, visionary, is you.
    The plague is you.

OEDIPUS: Of course.
    It was stupid of me not to see.
    It's jealousy that drives you.
    Amongst the people, suffering, desperate for someone to blame you arrive, with your education and your sweet words, your false prophesy and you spread lies about me.
    You attack me.
    And you increase your influence.
    I won't let you get away with it.

TIRESIAS: I have no need to get away with anything.
    The truth continues to exist.
    Whatever you or I choose to do.

OEDIPUS: Is this what you pick up at university.
    Revolution.
    It's as well to keep your brothers and sisters in blind ignorance

35

working the land.

They pose no danger to themselves that way.

TIRESIAS: You, Oedipus, taught me everything I needed to know.

OEDIPUS: Did I, well. return the favour, teach me, in what way, exactly am I responsible for the plague.

TIRESIAS: You truly don't understand do you.

OEDIPUS: No. I'm ignorant. A shovel in the earth's the only thing I understand. I have no university degree. Tell me.

TIRESIAS: You — your existence — is killing my people.

OEDIPUS: Revolution spoken twice.

You'll serve a long sentence for this.

TIRESIAS: Do you want me to say more.

So you can have me executed?

OEDIPUS: Nothing would give me greater pleasure.

TIRESIAS: Let me tell you then, visionary, your have no idea of the crime that sits at the core of your existence.

You, your family and all those you care about

are mired in crime.

And you can't see it.

OEDIPUS: You think I wouldn't strike a blind man.

You think you're invulnerable.

TIRESIAS: I can be brought no lower than I am.

The truth is invulnerable.

The two GUARDS, at OEDIPUS's signal, restrain TIRESIAS. OEDIPUS approaches him.

OEDIPUS: And truth is all I care about so I won't listen to anymore of your poisonous lies. You know nothing. You're a powerless blind man. You rage against what you call injustice. But in reality, its just natural law.

TIRESIAS: And I pity you, visionary, for calling me by the very names that you'll answer to soon enough.

OEDIPUS walks away from TIRESIAS and returns to his house.

OEDIPUS: Live on in your darkness, lost in the same starless night you were born from. You can't harm me.

TIRESIAS: True. It's not my destiny to destroy you. Your destruction belongs to nature. Nature will destroy you.

OEDIPUS: These jewel words. Do they sound like words even a university educated savage could roll about his mouth? No. These words have been fed to you by someone else.

TIRESIAS: No one else. My words. Your fate.

OEDIPUS: Take him to the barn.
 I'll find out what I need tomorrow.

Scene 8

The marketplace. A crowd. TIRESIAS has been severely beaten during the night. He is kneeling, handcuffed, between two GUARDS. OEDIPUS stands over him.

OEDIPUS: Money, power, a good job, a swimming pool, a car.
 One man has them and the rest are sick with jealousy.
 Most men would kill for a life like mine.
 But I didn't ask for this life.
 I was given it.
 By nature.
 My knowledge, my skills, my hard work are what nature gave me but now it seems my brother, the one you call Creon

became so jealous of my success that he set this barrel of
words, this trader in lies, to undermine my reputation.

This mongrel creation may be blind, but I assure you he's got
an eye for easy money.

He talks enough but what did he ever actually do for you?

When the land was dry did he build a dam?

When you were plagued with criminals did he drive them away?

If he's so clever why didn't he do something then, when you
needed help?

Your blind performing monkey.

Your reader of entrails.

Your maker of potions.

Your witch was useless to you until I turned up.

Stupid, visionary, Oedipus.

I saw what needed done and I did it.

Is it so hard for you to understand that a human saved you?

Not gods, or spirits, or fetishes or lucky charms.

Now you reward me by listening to the lazy accusations of a
scheming, power hungry, gangster.

Don't you see? He's in Creon's pocket, adviser of a drunk.

You think if Creon was your boss with this pie dog barking
orders you'ld be better off?

You deserve plague.

**OEDIPUS takes a riding crop and lashes TIRESIAS across
the face. TIRESIAS doesn't scream.**

OEDIPUS: Your prophet didn't prophesy that did he?

I ought to whip his arse over the mountains for him.

KING: I suggest his words were spoken in anger, sir, and your
response is too quick.

Thrashing around in anger and haste won't save our people
from drowning in their own blood. Sir, we need calm heads to
steer us to safety.

TIRESIAS: Visionary, you have power, but I'm your equal. I'm human too. I'm not your slave. Nor do I belong to Creon.

My words belong only to the truth.

I will speak freely.

You have mocked my blindness.

But your own precious eyes blind you to yourself.

You don't see the corruption of your own life.

That the house you live in is built out of murdered flesh.

That your swimming pool is filled with blood.

That your wife is smeared in shame.

That your children are unnatural creations.

Those of us left alive, and those of us dead will one day pick up the lash of your own curses and whip you from this land.

You'll stagger terrified with bleeding eyes to look for mercy.

And there will be none.

And you'll scream for pity.

And the mountains and the rocks and the sky will send back only the empty echo of your own anguish.

And you will curse the voice that sent you here to this land.

You'll curse the compass that guided you to this fatal shore.

You'll curse the chance that one day led you to choose one road over another and make this untameable place your home.

This? Your home?

And your children will look at you with disgust.

They'll reject you.

Those amongst our people you named as friends,

will turn their backs on you.

So call me what you want.

Mongrel, liar. Suspect your brother. Insult language.

Truth, whose words are balm on my parched lips, is my only concern.

Your suffering will be beyond mine one day when every smile, every kind word, every sunrise and every drunken evening of your life and every act of married love has turned to funeral ash in your memory.

OEDIPUS: I don't need to listen to this filth?
   Why is he still alive?

TIRESIAS: I told you the truth because you asked for it

OEDIPUS: If I'd known you'ld spew out venom and lies I'd never
   have asked.

TIRESIAS: Your education taught me to speak this way.
   It's your language I use.

OEDIPUS: You do love to parade your knowledge don't you.

TIRESIAS: Aren't you the great intelligence? Visionary.
   Don't you engineer dams, and roads.
   Tamer of nature.

OEDIPUS: Mock vision. Vision is what gives me power.

TIRESIAS: That gift made you and in time that gift will destroy you.

OEDIPUS: And it will save your people.
   Who cares what effect it has on me.

TIRESIAS: I have no more to say to you.
   I dismiss you from my presence.

OEDIPUS: Kill him.
   Before I lose control and kill him myself.

Scene 9

CHORUS. Evening. A group of wealthy women and men, around the swimming pool. Food cooking on a barbecue. Beers.

CHORUS: I can't say it
   Say it.
   It's criminal and perverse.

Say it.

I can't. It can't be said It's.

Unspeakable.

The accusation.

Who? Who? Tell.

I tell you this.

Whoever it was he's got blood on his hands.

He'll be running now.

He'll be running till his lungs burst.

He'll be running faster than a mountain gale.

Like lightning.

And there'll be police, armed police, on his tail.

Dogs.

Bold. hungry dogs tearing at his heels.

Barking and roaring.

And tearing his criminal skin with razor teeth.

He left no trace, you know.

He's cunning.

A very knowledgeable, wicked form of a criminal.

But Justice tore the sky open with the sound of her command.

Catch him.

He rests in barns, in caves, in rock piles.

He runs at night.

In the slippery course of mountain streams.

Trying to throw the dogs off his scent.

But he's given away by the vultures.

Who circle above his head.

He's breathing but he's already a dead man.

And those vulture's smell his terror.

The black wings swoop down and envelop his head.

Those talons pick out his eyes.

It's scary.

To think a killer and a murderer was living in our township.

The natives say it was —

Their man, their spokesman said it was —

No.
Oedipus.
They're liars by nature.
No smoke.
No ash.
Without a fire so.
But no.
I'm not saying I know what happened.
I'm not saying I know what's going to happen.
But Oedipus?
There was no bad blood between us and Corinth?
I've never heard a bad word spoken of Oedipus.
The natives love him.
They're loyal to him. Fiercely loyal.

God knows.
Life's a mystery.
Still waters run deep.
A man's heart is beyond seeing.
And they have no proof.
When mobs start shouting accusations, I say – show me the evidence.
But whatever he's done.
Killer or not.
He made this land fertile.
He built the dam and brought the road.
To us at least
he'll always be a hero.

Scene 10

CREON arrives at the barbecue. Drunk looking. He has a gun visible in a holster at his waist. The guests fall silent.

CREON: I hear the boss was calling me names.

No; don't stop, drink. I'm only asking.

Called me a cunt

Didn't he? Isn't that what he said?

Called me . . .

It hurts. You know. It truly does.

These are bad times, and I've been racking my brains because bad times are bad times and . . . really, struggling to think if anything I've done, or said could have been misinterpreted, or taken the wrong way you know so that he might think I'm treacherous.

Which is what the boys told me he said, in the marketplace, in front of the natives which . . .

Puts me in a very difficult position.

Because I'm going to find it hard to get respect from the staff now. And not just the staff because I can see you all.

You're all looking at me and thinking . . .

Maybe he is, if the boss says he is, maybe he really is.

A treacherous little cunt

MAN 1: As far as I heard he may have said something but –

You know he was angry.

He probably just, got his words muddled up out of anger.

CREON: Yes. I think you must be right

Because, just so I can be sure, he did say that I paid the prophet man to spread propaganda.

WOMAN 1: I think something like that was said by someone.

I don't know if there was any intention behind it .

CREON: But he did say these words, in public, am I right?

And he wasn't drunk or mad at the time?

MAN 2: I really couldn't confirm that. I wasn't there.

And you know. He's a great man, Creon, he –

WOMAN 2: Must have reasons to say things which we can't know.

OEDIPUS arrives on the step, from the house.

OEDIPUS: The murderer turns up at the gates of the dead man's house.

> That takes gall.
> But then it takes gall to plan to kill your own brother in law so you can own the land he's farmed. The wealth he's made.
> Tell me, Creon.
> Did you think I was blind?
> Did you take me for a fucking idiot?
> Or maybe you thought when I caught you I'd pity you?
> Not actually cut you open.
> It seems you've been the fool.
> You're a farm labourer Creon.
> No better.
> And now your swimming far out of your depth.
> Legs kicking, head sinking.
> What on earth made you think you could defeat me.
> You need money, brains, skills, men to take me on.

CREON: Boss, this is hard for me to bear, hearing these accusations.
> But if you say so boss it must be true.
> I'm only asking you. Because I'm a labourer, like you say.
> I can't follow the logical leaps a clever man like you can make.
> Show me the facts.
> Because I want to believe you. I really do.

OEDIPUS: You anger me Creon.
> You always did.
> I find your continuing presence here is making me angry.
> I think you ought to leave.

CREON: Can I just say, Boss.

OEDIPUS: Please don't whimper at me Creon.
> Don't beg.

CREON: You're off your head. You're diseased.
    You've taken the plague inside your brain and it's spreading.
    You're unbalanced.

OEDIPUS: Just because I'm related to you.
    Doesn't mean I wont kill you.

CREON: What the fuck am I supposed to have done?

OEDIPUS: How long ago did Laius . . .

CREON: What's Laius got to do with me . . .

OEDIPUS: Disappear. Die. Murdered on the road.

CREON: A long time ago.

OEDIPUS: And did the natives have prophets then?

CREON: Of course they did.

OEDIPUS: Did any of them mention my name.
    Casually.
    'Oedipus did it'
    Was that a thing they divined from ashes?

CREON: No. Not that I heard of.

OEDIPUS: But you did investigate the disappearance?
    Of your then brother in law.

CREON: We tried but . . . we got nowhere.

OEDIPUS: No evidence pointed to a man with a limp or anything?
    There's nothing you're keeping back is there?

CREON: I don't know.
    And when I don't know the facts.
    I don't speak.

OEDIPUS: But you do know this fact don't you.
    You killed one brother in law.
    Only to find another took his place.

And then you thought you'ld get rid of him.
By whipping up the natives against me.

CREON: Now can I ask you a question.

You married my sister, didn't you?

OEDIPUS: Detective now?

CREON: And it's your land. Yours and hers. In joint name.

OEDIPUS: A bit late now to start detecting isn't it?

CREON: This logic's obvious. But you don't see it.
What sane man would want the pressures of running this land.
The dangers, the anxieties, the stress of farming this desperate
territory when he could sleep easily in his bed at night, drive
a nice car and drink without any worries.
Only a boss.
A man with something to prove. Driven, you might say.
Not me.
I'm lazy. I'm drunk. Look at my life.
I do fuck all.
And I get paid.
If I'm hungry you feed me. If I'm bored I go to the city and
spend your money on whores.
If I was boss I'd drown In the fucking paperwork.
Why would I want any more than what I've got.
Nobody complains to me, everyone likes me.
The locals suck up to me, buy me beer and present their wives
to me, because they know I can influence you.
So why should I want to give it all up to get rid of you?
I know my limits Oedipus.
I have no taste for real power
I'm a coward and a bully.
I'm a brother in law by nature, I'm designed this way.
Go to the capital.
Ask anyone.

If they tell you I'm a liar.
Kill me.
But don't waste your energy on this stupid paranoia.
I'm no threat to you.

WOMAN 3: He's got a point.
If you jump to conclusions.
You stumble.

CREON: Do you want me to go?

OEDIPUS: I want you dead.

CREON: You're sure about that?

OEDIPUS: You don't believe me?

CREON: I think you're out of your fucking mind.
He wants to kill me.
You heard him.
Listen to him.

OEDIPUS: I'm listening to my own good sense.

CREON: What if you're wrong.

OEDIPUS: It doesn't matter. I have the right to act in self defence.

CREON: Not when there isn't a threat

OEDIPUS: This is my land.

CREON: It's my land too.

MAN 1: Stop. Both of you.
I've brought Jocasta.

WOMAN 1: Just in time.

MAN 1: Your wife and your sister

WOMAN 2: Lets see if she can settle anything

JOCASTA: You should be ashamed.

Both of you.

I don't know what to say.

We haven't got time for petty feuding.

The plague's on our doorstep and the township's on the edge of riot. The land's barren and you two arguing like children.

Go home Creon and sober up.

And you.

Inside.

CREON: Sister, listen to me.

You've got to do something about your lunatic husband.

He's talking about arresting me. Having me killed.

OEDIPUS: I caught him out

He was plotting against both of us.

CREON: Never.

CREON puts his gun in OEDIPUS' hand.

CREON: I swear to god.

I swear to all gods everywhere.

I swear on my life.

If I've done-anything wrong.

Kill me.

Let me be damned to hell.

JOCASTA: In the name of god believe him.

He's standing there, drunk.

He's offering his life to you.

Respect the man's courage.

These people believe him.

I believe him.

Why can't you?

WOMAN 3: Listen to her.

Give it up.

Please.

OEDIPUS: What do you want from me?

MAN 3: Have some pity for Creon. He's one of us.
    He's never caused trouble before.
    And look at him.

WOMAN: I admire him.

WOMAN 3: He's a brave man.

OEDIPUS: You want me to back down?

MAN 2: Yes.

OEDIPUS: Then tell me precisely what you want me to do.
    You're in charge.

MAN 2: The man's your brother in law. He's your friend.
    And he's sworn on his own life that he's innocent.
    Surely you don't believe the word of natives against one of us.

OEDIPUS: Either he's a traitor or I am a killer.
    You're saying you believe I killed Laius.

CHORUS: We're not saying that.
    God send daylight.
    Night darkness and fear are making these minds drunk.
    This country's sick.
    And this argument's upsetting my stomach.
    I can't bear it.

OEDIPUS: Let him go.
    Let me be ruined.
    I can't argue with sentimentality.
    I have no pity for him.
    Wherever he goes he takes my hate.

CREON: Oedipus.
    You're a lost soul.

A cornered animal.

Showing your claws, your heart double thumping in fear.

I've no need to look for justice.

To know you inhabit your own snakepit mind is my revenge.

OEDIPUS: Leave me alone. All of you.

Get out.

Get out!

CREON: I'm going. I'm going to the capital.

You never knew me.

You're a foreigner.

My people understand me.

I'll always have a home here.

You don't even understand yourself.

You're wandering lost.

Goodbye boss.

You'll find the truth eventually and then your conscience will shatter what's left of your sanity.

CREON leaves.

WOMAN 4: You should take him inside. He needs to calm down.

JOCASTA: What did they say to each other?

CHORUS: You should have heard it.

A cloud of foul words and flying accusations.

It's very sad.

JOCASTA: From both of them?

CHORUS: Oh yes.

JOCASTA: Who started it?

CHORUS: Don't ask.

Enough.

Please.

This plagues tearing at the heart of everything.
It's cut open scars.
And picked at scabs.
Leave it alone.

OEDIPUS: See where your tearful sentiments have got you. You're all desperate to ignore the truth. Look at yourselves, your self indulgent weeping over Creon blurs your sight and blunts your anger. We need to be ruthless. We must show no mercy.

CHORUS: Oedipus.
You're a good man.
We're not stupid enough to think we know better than you.
We're only human.
You took a shattered country and healed it once.
We trust you to look after us.
Don't let us down.

Scene 11

Darkness. The lights of fires from the township. OEDIPUS, sitting where he was. JOCASTA near him.

JOCASTA: Come to bed.
Don't ignore me.
In the township they're burning the shacks.
The smell's keeping me awake.
It's frightening.
Don't leave me alone tonight.

OEDIPUS: He said I killed Laius. He said I did it.

JOCASTA: He didn't say that.

OEDIPUS: He didn't say it himself.

He put the words in the mouth of one of their prophets.
One of their filthy rabble rousers.

JOCASTA: Listen to me.

The people have their prophesies, their rituals of seeing and they're colourful. Nothing more. But, if you allow yourself to worry about them, then images, ideas, enter your head and take control of you. It's a primitive force, it's part of the night. It feels strong, Oedipus but it's a hollow power.

Laius used to love the people and he let himself be seduced by their religion. After our first baby was born he went to a prophet to have the future told for him. The old priest burnt offerings and looked at the sky and rolled bones and read the skin on the baby's body and then he said.

'Your son will kill you'.

He told Laius.

'Your son will kill you'.

And so . . .

So my son . . .

This is the nature of this place and if you're seduced by it you become savage yourself.

My son, who was barely three days old . . .

I remember holding his head against me and he was searching for my breast. Pushing and pushing. Still blind but searching and . . .

My husband took him from my arms.

And I watched and he . . .

Put nails through the screaming boy's ankles and . . .

Laius gave my baby to a herdboy to take to the mountains and told him to leave him there, exposed on the rocks, to be taken by animals.

My baby didn't murder his father.

Laius died in a car crash at the crossroads.

His driver was drunk.

The old prophet was nothing more than a dream merchant.

But he tore my boy away from me.
And had him killed.
So clean your mind of that darkness.
Think clearly. In daylight.
Let whatever happens happen.
You won't find answers at night.

OEDIPUS: Jocasta
Tell me you're lying.
Tell me this story's made up to soothe me.

JOCASTA: I'm not lying.

OEDIPUS: Laius died in a car crash at a crossroads?

JOCASTA: That's what we were told.

OEDIPUS: Where. Exactly where?

JOCASTA: Phocis.

OEDIPUS: When?

JOCASTA: A few months before you arrived.
In the middle of the drought.
Before you built the dam and we . . .

OEDIPUS: God. God.
What sort of black nightmare am I walking into.

JOCASTA: What are you saying?
Oedipus you're frightening me.

OEDIPUS: What if the blind prophet isn't blind?

JOCASTA: I told you not to worry about . . .

OEDIPUS: How did Laius travel?
Did he take men with him? Was he armed?

JOCASTA: He took some men. I'm sure they had guns.
They took one of the trucks.

OEDIPUS: It's the middle of the night but I can see as clearly as if
it was mid-day. The sun's come up. I'm burning. I'm burning
alive. Jocasta, who told you this?

JOCASTA: The houseboy,
He was the only one who survived the attack.

OEDIPUS: Which houseboy. One of ours?

JOCASTA: No.
He left.
When you and I got married he said he couldn't stay.
The memory of Laius was too much for him.
I gave him some money and he left.
He loved Laius. He was always loyal to him.
He deserved money.

OEDIPUS: Can he be contacted?

JOCASTA: I think so. I'm sure one of them will know where he is.
Why?

OEDIPUS: Find him.
Now.
Do it.

JOCASTA: If you want him found I'll see he's found.
But you're worried. You look sick.
Tell me.
What's wrong with you?
Tell queen.

OEDIPUS: I'm frightened,
Not for the first time.
Let me lay my head on your chest.
Hold me.
There's no one else I can tell.

JOCASTA: Tell me.

OEDIPUS: On our lands near Corinth, where I grew up.

    The local people had a prophet, they'd go to him for cures and advice.

    He was a fat man, rolls of fat hung from under his shirt.

    My friends and I would mock him, call him names.

    And he ignored us.

    But one day when I was nearly eighteen and one of the leaders of the city.

    I was at a party.

    And one of my friends, my friend of a long time.

    Called me a bastard.

    He was drunk.

    But I knew he wasn't joking.

    I knew he was letting something out.

    Drink was making him talk.

    'You're not your father's son'. He said. Straight at me.

    None of my other friends backed me up.

    They looked at me. Waiting for a response.

    I left.

    I walked through the night towards home but I couldn't clear my head. I found myself in the local village.

    And I found myself at the door of the prophet's hut.

    He told me to come in.

    Our people would never visit the village, especially at night, but he didn't seem surprised to see me.

    I sat on the earth floor and I asked him what he saw in my past and what he saw in my future.

    He burned offerings, he looked at the stars, he rolled bones and he read my skin.

    And he told me he could see my future and he could see my past. I said. 'Am I my father's son?'

    And he said.

    'Yes.'

    And I said, 'prophet, what do you see?'

    He said.

'You will kill your father.

And you will fuck your mother.'

JOCASTA: No.

OEDIPUS: He made me see.

In that black night, in his hut, the smell of smoke and the sound of the fire, his voice, his fat skin he made me see the horror of my life.

I didn't go home that night.

I walked through the village and the people all came from their huts to watch me walk down the muddy track.

And I saw pity in their eyes.

I was their master.

But I knew they would rather have been the most savagely beaten hungry slave than be me.

I walked to the main road.

And I walked away from Corinth.

Away from the fat prophet's vision.

I didn't stop.

I walked for months as though I was in a dream.

I sat on beaches for days on end and watched the sea.

I starved myself.

I got drunk with criminals in shebeens.

I studied scriptures with wandering monks.

I walked.

And one day, near Phocis, I came to a crossroads.

And I couldn't decide which way to go.

Each road seemed exactly the same.

I was tired. I wanted to stop moving forward. But I knew I couldn't go back.

And then a truck approached me on the road.

I didn't have the energy or will to move out of the way.

At that moment I wanted to die.

I stood still.

I thought, let nature take it's course.

The driver swerved and the truck went into a ditch.

There was silence.

And. Insects and then . . .

A single man, clawed his way out of the wreckage and onto the grass at the side of the road.

He was covered in blood but he was alive.

He looked at me.

And his eyes were

Full of sorrow.

But I left him.

I couldn't bring myself to feel even pity.

(Pause)

I can still see it.

Jocasta —

I told the people in the marketplace to give the killer nothing.

If I killed Laius.

Then I'm nothing.

I made the law for my own punishment.

(Pause)

I touched your pure skin with these hands, Jocasta.

Killer hands.

So now I have to exile myself. Again.

It seems there's no patch of land on this earth prepared to let me make a home.

Each place I live must eventually spew me out.

To cure itself of disease.

I'm killer.

I'm mass murder.

Is there a god so drunk with hate that he could plan this for a man? For me?

Is there enough cruelty in nature that an evil birth like mine could happen?

Did no god have the pity to tear the sky apart on the day of my conception and spit death into my mother's womb?

That womb made out of ashes and blood. Was there not

enough pity in nature to let me meet the earth stillborn?
(Pause)
Dawn.
Don't let it come.
I'm night covered now. Night over me.
Night in me.

JOCASTA: Oedipus.
The story's awful.
But . . .
Maybe . . . hope. There's hope still if . . .
Until we meet the houseboy, he saw, we don't know.

OEDIPUS: He's my hope.
Waiting.
Till he comes from the mountains.

JOCASTA: He saw. He's a witness.

OEDIPUS: If the driver was drunk like you say.
Then I'm not killer.
If the driver saw me.
I'm killer.

JOCASTA: He really did say 'drunk'.
Everyone heard him, not just me.
That's the story he told.
He can't change his story now,
and even if he does. Oedipus?
It still proves nothing about that horrible prophet.
A prophet said Laius would be killed by my baby.
But my baby died.
Prophesies, just lies, superstition and coincidence.
The future's shapeless and meaningless and . . .
We make it ourselves.
We create it

OEDIPUS: My only hope's the houseboy.

Bring him.

JOCASTA: Come to bed now.
   You're tired.
   Come with me.
   Let me hold you.
   Let me comfort you.

Scene 12

Dawn. A patch of earth by a dry river bed. CHORUS kneeling. PRIEST preaching.

CHORUS: Nature
   Purify us.
   Guide us.
   Surround us.
   Sustain us.
   Rule us.

PRIEST: Life comes from the earth.
   Thought enters us inbreathed from air.
   Work is made by soil, water and light.
   Words are made of smoke from night fires.
   Man is nothing.

CHORUS: His words are nothing.
   His laws are nothing.
   Nature is everything.

PRIEST: A man thinks he has power.
   Pride blinds him.
   He rises over us.
   Higher than grass, higher than trees, higher than vultures,
   higher even than the mountains.

He looks down on us.
And then he sees nothing beneath his feet.
No earth to hold his weight.
And he falls.
Proud blind power.
Falls out of the sky.

CHORUS: Nature shatters all human power.
Bones crushed to dust.

PRIEST: Build houses.
Farm land.
Make money.
Enforce laws.
Think well of yourself.
But you are nothing to nature.
You will fall.
You will find your life in pieces.
You will be broken.
You will be smashed.

CHORUS: Nature shatters all human power.

PRIEST: So we gather and kneel in the dust.
Humbly.
And beg for mercy.

CHORUS: Faith.
Prophecy.
Prayer.
And Ritual.
Immerse us, for one moment, in nature.
Our minds and bodies dissolve.
We become everything.
We become all time.
We are ashes.
And we are the memory of fire.

The faithless.
Breathe in darkness.
They die.
Unborn.

Scene 13

A dark hut. A shaft of bright daylight from the small hut doorway. JOCASTA and the PRIEST sit. The PRIEST arranges a newspaper. He pours a tin cup of water in a circle. He sets light to the paper. It bums out. He looks at the ashes.

JOCASTA: My husband is lost.
He's lost his footing.
The past is darkness to him and the future darkness.
There's no light in his mind.
He's made of fear.
He's beyond my reach.
Please.
Purify us.
Guide us.
Surround us.
Sustain us.
Please.
We're afraid.
Comfort us.

Scene 14

Daylight. The swimming pool. The CHORUS behind razor wire. A man arrives, he speaks to the two armed GUARDS.

MESSENGER: I'm looking for a man called Oedipus.

GUARD: This is his house.

JOCASTA enters.

JOCASTA: Who are you? What do you want?

MESSENGER: I've come from Corinth. Do you live here?

JOCASTA: Yes.

MESSENGER: This is a beautiful house madam.

JOCASTA: What do you want with us?

MESSENGER: I've got a message for Oedipus I'm an old friend
of his

JOCASTA: Tell me the message.
Oedipus is sick. He can't be disturbed.
Is it bad news?

MESSENGER: Its news. Good, bad. Who knows?

JOCASTA: Don't play with words grandad. Tell me.

MESSENGER: Oedipus has come into his inheritance.
His land in Corinth needs a farmer.
His family want him to return.
So that's good isn't it.

JOCASTA: His father farms the land.

MESSENGER: I know but his father's dead.
That's the bad aspect of the news.

JOCASTA: How?

MESSENGER: The poor man had a heart attack.

JOCASTA: **(to GUARD)** Get master. Bring him now.
This is good news. Good news.
(To CHORUS)

62

Where's prophecy now?
He died alone.
He died naturally.
Oedipus didn't kill him.
Did you hear that?
Natural causes.
(To MESSENGER)
You're not lying are you?

MESSENGER: No.

OEDIPUS comes out.

OEDIPUS: Why did you call me?

JOCASTA: This man, Oedipus, he's come from Corinth.
    The prophesies, they're empty Oedipus.
    We're free.
    Your father's dead.

OEDIPUS: Let me hear him say it.

MESSENGER: Polybus, your father, is dead.

OEDIPUS: How, murder, sickness what?

MESSENGER: He was an old man. He had a heart attack.

OEDIPUS: My poor father
    Was he ill for long?

MESSENGER: He was old.
    One morning he walked out into the sunshine and fell.
    He felt very little.
    The farm in Corinth belongs to you now.

OEDIPUS: Why? Why? Jocasta. Look at us.
    Why did we spend time with our hands scrabbling in prophet's
    ash, listening to the rubbish talked by old native men.
    'You will kill your father', he said.

The man's dead and I never touched him.
Never came near him.
He's dead and he's taken the prophesies with him.
They're in the ground with him.
And the memory of that dark hut, the memory of those terrible
words, burned away, Jocasta, smoke on the wind.

JOCASTA: Didn't I tell you.

OEDIPUS: You were right.

Fear turned me mad.
Of course you were right.

JOCASTA: Nothing to fear
Nothing at all.
We make the future.
It's a step away from us.
Out of sight of prophets or anyone else.

OEDIPUS: But my mother. The prophet said . . .

JOCASTA: He was playing on your fears.
A man's worst fear is that the thought of his mother creeps
unasked for into his mind while he fucks his wife.
The prophets use that fear.
It's obvious. The man's a charlatan.
See him for what he is.
Playing games with your mind.
That's all.
You should be happy.
Bring this man in. Give him food and drink.
We should celebrate Oedipus.
Tomorrow's nothing to us.
You're free again.

Scene 15

Night. Around the pool. OEDIPUS and JOCASTA. The MESSENGER. The light of fires from the township. Beer.

JOCASTA: More beer? Take more. You're welcome.

MESSENGER: Thankyou.

OEDIPUS: You've had a long journey.

MESSENGER: I wanted to come here.
I asked especially for the job. Even though I'm old.
I wanted to see you again.
I told your wife I was an old friend but I don't suppose you remember me.

OEDIPUS: I'm sorry but there were so many servants and it was so long ago.

MESSENGER: This house, and all this land, your reputation.
I'm very proud of you.
You're a powerful man.
Very proud.

OEDIPUS: You're very kind.

MESSENGER: I might be a little drunk.
I'm – I shouldn't but – you know –
You upset us. When you left.
You ran away and
There was a lot of sadness in Corinth.

OEDIPUS: I had to leave.

MESSENGER: Why? Why? Everyone loved you there was no reason to run.

OEDIPUS: It was a difficult time.

MESSENGER: We were confused.

You didn't leave a message.
Nothing to give us comfort

OEDIPUS: I had an experience which made me afraid.
It was nothing.
But it seemed terrifying at the time.

MESSENGER: You – frightened. I can't believe it.

OEDIPUS: It's true.

MESSENGER: Put my mind at rest. I've known you since you were
a tiny baby. Sir, tell me.

OEDIPUS: The prophet in Corrinth told me, one night, the night
before I left that I was destined to kill my father.

MESSENGER: But you didn't

OEDIPUS: I know.
I know that now.
But the fear of it lived with me, the terror of what I might do.
What I might be capable of.
I had to run away.

MESSENGER: Life. I'm an old man.
The cruelty of life. The tricks it plays.
I've had too much of your beer but I must tell you –
Because I'm proud of you –
You didn't need to run away.
Anyone in the household could have told you, if you'ld only
asked. Polybus wasn't your real father.
You were adopted.

OEDIPUS: No. He called me son. He was my father.

MESSENGER: He loved you like a son. You were a son to him but
Oedipus, more than a son. You were a gift to him from me.

OEDIPUS: From you? What, did you buy me in the market?
You're drunk.

MESSENGER: I found you, Oedipus, screaming amongst the rocks in the mountains near here. Cithairon. I was a herdboy then, a young man, and your crying was hard to bear but I couldn't resist you. And what they'd done to you. Oedipus, it was horrible. Your feet were nailed together. You were lucky to be still alive. I took pity on you. I took you in to the mountain hut where I stayed with the other herdboys. We gave you milk from the sheep and gently took the nails from your feet. We nursed you, us boys, until the season was over and I carried you back with me to Corinth. Tied in a blanket on my back like a woman! I was your first mother. It must be hard to hear this story but, to see you here, you understand, it makes me proud.

OEDIPUS: God. God, No.
     Jocasta what's he saying.
     Who did this to me.
     My mother?
     My father?

MESSENGER: I don't know.
     You'ld need to ask the other herdboy.

JOCASTA: Which one?

MESSENGER: One of Laius'. He brought the baby to the mountain. It was him that gave you to me.

OEDIPUS: Is he alive? Who is he. This herdboy?

MESSENGER: **(pointing at the fires)** I can't tell you but they'll know in the township if you ask.

OEDIPUS: I'll ask. I'll ask.

JOCASTA: What man? What herdboy? This is nonsense Oedipus.
     This old man's fantasising.
     Forget this. leave it.

MESSENGER: I'm telling the truth.

JOCASTA: You're a liar.

A poisonous liar.

You drink our beer and you spew out lies.

(To GUARDS) Get rid of him. Take him away.

MESSENGER: I'm sorry madam.

I'm telling the truth.

JOCASTA: Not another word or I'll have them whip you.

Take him to the road.

The GUARDS take the MESSENGER away.

JOCASTA: Forget this. Oedipus. It's nothing but drunken dreams.

OEDIPUS: Forget it?

I don't know who I am?

How can I . . .

JOCASTA: No. Leave it.

No more questions.

For your own sake.

I'm asking you.

For my sake.

Think what this knowledge is doing to me.

Leave it alone.

OEDIPUS: I see.

It's clear enough. You can't hide it.

You're ashamed of me.

Now you discover that I might be one of them.

The son of some herdboy.

The son of some poor native woman.

Probably the bastard child of a master.

A halfbreed.

You want me out.

JOCASTA: Please stop this.

I'm begging you.
Stop.

OEDIPUS: I have to know.
Naturally I have to know who I am.

JOCASTA: This isn't natural. I promise.

OEDIPUS: Fuck nature then.

JOCASTA: Oedipus. Oedipus.
Please.
Let this stay buried.

OEDIPUS: **(to a GUARD)** Take me to the township. We'll find the herdboy the old man was talking about.
Leave me alone, Jocasta, you obviously don't want to humiliate yourself by talking to a native man.
Am I still your husband.
Or can't you bring yourself to call me that?

JOCASTA: There's no name to . . .
No word to . . .
Oedipus.
Pity . . .
The only word . . .
Pity pity pity pity.

JOCASTA exits in distress.

OEDIPUS: Let it all come out Let it all come pouring out.
I will uncover myself.
Native born, rape born, born in shame I don't care.
She's a woman, she's worried about appearances.
About gossip and talk.
She's afraid of what I might discover.
But I'm mother nature's son, and I have a right to my inheritance.

Nothing natural can be wrong.
I'm unshameable.
Bare rock and cold sky nursed me, and luck, my brother luck,
grew up beside me.
Luck led me, luck carved my mind.
Made me myself.
My blood my nature drive me.
I have to find my parents.

Scene 16

The marketplace. Night. OEDIPUS stands in the middle drinking, happy. The CHORUS surround him. Firelight.

CHORUS: If I know anything.
Prophet knowledge is beyond me.
But I can guess and I guess that
Oedipus, tomorrow, will come with us and we'll give thanks to the mountains.
Mountain mother who saved him.
Mountain mother who made him.
Oedipus, one of us, Oedipus born poor.
And we'll carry him to the foothills.
We'll sing, we'll dance, we'll sacrifice and we'll initiate him into our tribe.
He'll be one of us.
Oedipus.
Son of us.
Who made you?
Which of the laughing river spirits fucked with the god of goats.
Or was it a wild herdboy, who raped a lonely tourist in her tent.
No, no it was lighting. Lighting fucked a tree and there was fire.
Fire.

And Oedipus was made from smoke and ash.
It was drunk god, drunk god dancing on hilltops.
His cock dragging the earth.
Found it's way into a cave.
And he impregnated the mountain herself.
That's what happened.
And you were born in an earthquake.
And drunk god looked in your baby eyes and blessed you.
Little son of mine.
He said.
And the fumes of his drunk breath intoxicated the whole country for a thousand years.

The laughter and excitement calms down as it is realised that an old man, the HERDBOY is standing at the edge of the crowd, two GUARDS are nearby. OEDIPUS stands next to the MESSENGER.

OEDIPUS. At a guess, I'd say this lonely man, hiding in the shadows, is the herdboy with the secrets.
He's old enough, old grandad boy.
The pair of you are like grandad brothers.
Is he the man?

KING: I know him. This was one of Laius' men.
He was one of Laius' favourites.

OEDIPUS: Grandad! Come out of the shadows.
Look at me.
Answer me.
Were you Laius' man?
Herdboy?

HERDBOY: . . .

OEDIPUS: Answer me herdboy.
Did you work for Laius.

HERDBOY: I was his servant. I grew up with him.

OEDIPUS: What work did you do?

HERDBOY: Cattle work.

OEDIPUS: Where did you graze. What range?

HERDBOY: Cithairon. Mostly.

OEDIPUS: **(Referring to the MESSENGER)**
This old man. Do you know him?

HERDBOY: Why?

OEDIPUS: Because I'm asking.

HERDBOY: I don't know.

MESSENGER: No wonder he doesn't remember. It's years ago and in his memory I'm a young man, not the old relic in front of him now. But if I tell you I grazed my flocks on Cithairon, and we shared the mountain hut every summer with the other boys. If I say I died my hair the colour of flame red and I carried a knife. If I mention the time we got pissed on homebrew and lost half our flock in the gully below the vulture's nest and we spent two days searching together. Then come the end of summer we'd say goodbye and I'd go back south, him to Laius' fields. Do you remember now.

HERDBOY: I suppose. It's a long time ago.

MESSENGER: You remember a baby boy.
That summer, the boy you brought to me.
You said I could have him for my own.

HERDBOY: What if I do know you. Why have I been brought here? I committed no crime.

MESSENGER: That baby boy turned out to be Oedipus! The very man. The dambuilder and roadmaker and the most powerful man in the country! Can you believe it!

HERDBOY: Why don't you keep your fucking mouth shut.

OEDIPUS: Watch your tongue old man.
   I'll have you whipped.

HERDBOY: Why? What am I supposed to have done?

OEDIPUS: Just answer this man's question.
   Do you remember the baby boy?

HERDBOY: He knows nothing.

Enraged, OEDIPUS whips the old man's face. The two GUARDS hold the HERDBOY.

HERDBOY: Don't hurt me. Please. I'm an old man.

OEDIPUS: Talk!
   Hold him tight.

OEDIPUS whips his face again.

HERDBOY: Oedipus Oedipus!
   I feel sorry for you.
   What more do you need to know?

OEDIPUS: Did you give this man a child?

HERDBOY: I did.
   And I wish to god I'd died that day.

OEDIPUS: If you don't tell me everything.
   You will be dead.

HERDBOY: I'd rather die than tell.

OEDIPUS: He won't answer
   Take him to the barn.
   Give him a proper beating.
   He turns to walk away.

HERDBOY: I told you I gave him the child.

OEDIPUS: Who gave it to you? Was it yours . . . who?

HERDBOY: The child wasn't mine.

OEDIPUS: Someone here? Point Tell.

HERDBOY: Master I beg you.
    Please don't ask me that question.

OEDIPUS casually takes out a pistol. He places it, cocked, at the head of the MESSENGER.

OEDIPUS: If I have to ask you one more time.
    Your old friend will be dead.

HERDBOY: The child was born in Laius' house,

OEDIPUS: A native, a servant child or Laius' own?

HERDBOY: I can't say this . . .
    Pity.
    The words are . . .
    Pity. Pity. Pity.

OEDIPUS: Tell me who I am.

HERDBOY: The child was Laius' own.
    Ask you wife.
    She knows.

OEDIPUS: Laius gave you the child?

HERDBOY: Yes.

OEDIPUS: Why?

HERDBOY: He wanted the child killed.
    The prophesy demanded it.

OEDIPUS: What prophesy?

HERDBOY: The son would kill the father.
    The son would fuck the mother.

OEDIPUS: But you didn't kill the baby.

HERDBOY: Because I pitied him Master.
    I had pity.
    My pity saved him.
    Nursed him.
    And now.
    If you are Oedipus.
    If you are Oedipus.
    Then you must be made of pain.
    After silence.
    The first rays of dawn sunlight.

OEDIPUS: Night's going.
    Sun's coming.
    No.
    Night. Black hiding me night stay.
    Never take darkness away from me again.
    Let me hide drunk in night always.
    Blind drunk in utter blackness.
    Day is pain.
    Light is pain.
    Seeing is pain.
    Knowing is pain.
    The crime and the criminal the prophesy and the son are reunited in the same disgusting body.
    Me.
    This skin, this mind, this flesh is made of pain.

OEDIPUS leaves. All still. A considerable moment of silence. The priest speaks.

PRIEST: Parent becomes child.
    Child becomes parent.
    The one has been the other.
    The other will be the one.

And so on and so on beyond all imagining.
Against time we are nothing.
Smoke.
Utter silence.
Our life no more than the memory of the fire.
Contained in the ash.
In the circle of water.
We burn.
We make heat and light.
We consume ourselves.
Smoke.
Utter silence.
Ash.
Fasten your eyes to Oedipus.
We are him.
His life ours.
Limping, maimed, maddened and broken.
Made of pain.
What don't we know about ourselves?

In a single moment of terror
Oedipus was born.
We watched as he was immersed in nature.
Violently, without pity.
His mind and body dissolved.
He became nothing.
He became all time.
Nature shatters all humanity.
We are Oedipus.
We are nothing,
What can't we see?

WOMAN 1: My master.
Cruel, demanding, beautiful, kind and wise.
My master.
Dam builder Water giver.

Roadmaker. Farmer.
My master.
Your existence humiliated me.
Made me abject.
Made me a child again.
And I loved you.
Gave myself.
Covered you in the beaten gold of my love.
My master.
Is only a story of pain.
The body I nourished and cleaned has torn itself open.
The darkness inside him has poured into the world.
And the light of the sun.
Is sucked into the depths of his memory.
Reversed man.
My master.
Oedipus. Oedipus.
Smash ankled child
Visionary.

MAN 1: Someone tell me.
    How can the same cunt,
    the same deep wet cunt
    have room for the father and room for the son?
    Home cunt, safe cunt.
    A harbour against the storm of life.
    Cunt gives us comfort
    That's its job.
    But one at a time.
    Husband, father and son all together? No.
    How could cunt not dry up?
    Sew itself shut.
    Protest.
    To be so open.
    So unknowing.

Of it's own betrayal.

PRIEST: Dawn's come Oedipus and you are nothing to the dawn.
　　Dawn find's you fallen.
　　Your life in pieces.
　　Your heart broken.
　　Your mind in shreds.
　　Dawn finds you kneeling in the dust.
　　She lights you.
　　You beg for darkness.
　　But dawn shows no pity.
　　Nature shatters all human power.
　　Always.

WOMAN 1: I only wish.
　　My master.
　　I'd never seen you.
　　I grieve now.
　　I cry.
　　Sorrow. Sorrow.
　　Once you filled my eyes with light.
　　Now.
　　My eyes burn.

Scene 17

Daylight. The swimming pool stained deep red. The CHORUS behind razor wire. A SERVANT.

MAN 1: What happened here?

SERVANT: Jocasta is dead.
　　She's dead.

WOMAN 1: Poor woman, how? How did it happen?

SERVANT: Last night after Oedipus went to the township.
  She came calmly into the servant's quarters and asked for a
  knife. Of course we gave it to her.
  But I followed her and watched. I was worried.
  I saw her lying on her bed.
  Curled up.
  Silent as a stone.
  The knife held to her stomach.
  I waited. I didn't know what to do.
  And then.
  Soon after midnight.
  Suddenly.
  She screamed.
  It was a horrible sound. A scream of . . .
  Desolation.
  She tore at the bed with the knife.
  She pounded it with the knife, again and again until she
  was exhausted.
  And then she walked out here.
  She sat by the poolside.
  Her legs in the water.
  And she drew the knife to her stomach.
  And she cut into herself.
  She sat still, like a rock, and yet she-tore herself open.
  And then she slipped into the water.
  So quietly.
  Not a murmur of pain.
  But she was weeping. She was weeping with grief.
  Stillness.
  Stars.
  Dark.
  The household waiting.
  Till just after dawn when Oedipus returned.
  And he saw her lying in the pool.
  His wife.

Floating so gently on the water.
And he lowered himself into the pool.
And he walked towards her.
And he cradled her in his arms and lifted her from the water.
And he carried her into the house.
And he lay her on the bed.
And he took off her clothes.
And he looked at her ruined body.
And poor Oedipus.
He took her two gold brooch pins from her dress.
He held them in front of his face.
And he drove them into his eyes.
Again and again and again and again without pity.
Pulping his eyes.
Tearing them.
Blood and nerves and skin and socket ripped open over his face.
And still he said nothing.
Silence.
Not even a moan of pain.

OEDIPUS' voice from inside.

OEDIPUS: SHOW ME TO MY PEOPLE.
EXPOSE ME.
FATHER KILLER.
MOTHER FUCKER.
PLAGUE MAKER.
MAKE THEM SPIT.
MAKE THEM PISS IN MY WOUNDS.
SHOW ME TO THEM.
SHOW THEM THE CRIME.

OEDIPUS enters. His face bloody.

CHORUS: Look at the pain.

The pain in him.
As if he had found all the cruelty that exists nature, and
gathered it in a single act.
An act of hate beyond imagining.
Directed at himself.

OEDIPUS: I . . . I . . .
Where am I?
Am I still here?
Where's words?
Dust flying away from me?
Where can I find more pain.
To fill up what's left of my mind.
I still have room for thoughts of her.
Human thoughts.
Touching her.
Where can I escape?

KING: Oedipus you are in a place none of us can imagine.
We want to offer you some comfort.

OEDIPUS: If you want to comfort me. Torture me.
Let pain stave off the emptiness.
Dark cold emptiness filling my body.
Nothing can stop it coming.
I am.
Nothing.
My own voice.
Nothing voice.
Nothing words.
Nothing.
I am.
A moment of stillness on a road.
A womb torn wife.
And pulped eyes.

KING: Your grief, Oedipus, your remorse.

And your injuries are terrible.
Let us help you.

OEDIPUS: My friend. King?
Still my friend?
Is that your voice?
You still care for me?
What'll we talk about friend?
What conversation?
Old times, gossip, problems, plans.
It would be meaningless friend.
My friendship empty.
I can't offer you friendship.
I can only offer you my ruin.
Look at it in silence.
It's my gift

KING: How could you do this, attacking your own eyes.
How could you find the strength?

OEDIPUS: What use are eyes to me.
When all I can see is her ripped body.
What is there on earth that I could ever see that would give
me even the smallest amount of comfort.
Nothing.
I belong in darkness.
Take me away from here.
Now.
Lead me to the mountains.
To some cave.
Leave me there.
The most hated object in all nature.

KING: I pity you Oedipus.
You've suffered so much.
I wish you'ld never begun this search.
Some things it's better not to know.

OEDIPUS: No pity.

> Herdboy pity undid my nailed feet on Cithairon and saved me.
> Pity let me live. That was pity's kindness.
> I have killed pity.
> If there was true pity in the world,
> I would have died on the bare rock.
> My existence would not have been possible?
> But I am.
> I am here.
> I am Oedipus.
> The facts of my life.
> Father dead in the road.
> My sperm in my mothers cunt.
> My guilt become a cloud of plague to murder your children.
> If words could describe the crime, perhaps they could weave
> a blanket to cover them.
> To soften them.
> But no words.
> Only empty blackness in me.
> I am here.
> I am Oedipus.
> Look at me.
> Touch me.
> Don't be scared. You can touch me.
> Inside my skin is all the agony the world can make.
> I hold it in me.
> My skin protects you.
> Outside my skin the world is good.
> Touch me.

The CHORUS back away from the fence. OEDIPUS holds the razor wire. His hands cut and bloody. He retreats.

Scene 18

Evening. OEDIPUS, sitting by the still bloody swimming pool. Two GUARDS, also sitting, smoking, nearby. CREON enters with two CHILDREN.

OEDIPUS: Who is it? Who's there?

CREON: Creon.
    This is my land now, boss.
    My home.

OEDIPUS: What can I say to you.
    Sorry?

CREON: I'm not here to gloat
    Everything's finished.
    (To the GUARDS)
    You, you fucking savages.
    Have you no respect?
    Get a blanket
    Cover up this . . . this . . . sight.
    Take him inside.
    Gently.
    His grief belongs to us.
    His family.

OEDIPUS: Creon, please, take me away.
    You owe me nothing but please.
    Take me in the truck to somewhere far away.
    To a wilderness place.
    Leave me there.
    Please Creon.

CREON: You belong to us.
    You can stay here.

OEDIPUS: No. Creon.

Please.
Take me to Cithairon.
To the higher pastures.
Let me live there.
You must bury Jocasta.
Let me bury myself.
In the rocks.
Away.

CREON: This is still your house.
It turns out I'm a relative.
I'll give you shelter.
Obligation.

OEDIPUS: And the girls, Creon, my children.
You'll look after them.
You'll love them.
Care far them.
Won't you Creon.
Before I go you'll let me hold them.
If I could hold them to me.
Their warm shapes against me.
It would be as if nothing had happened.
As if nothing else were true.

CREON: They're here. I brought them with me.

OEDIPUS: You're kind Creon.
Kind.
Where are you children?
Come . . .
Come to me.
I'm your brother now. Your mother's my mother.
Look at my eyes.
Aren't they horrible.
Once I could see but I saw nothing.
Now I'm blind and can see everything.

I can see you so clearly.

Your lives . . .

Loves,

people will spit at you and whisper and stare.

Anywhere you go you'll leave in tears.

In school they'll be afraid of you.

When summer comes and the oranges are ripe.

No dancing women, no picking fruit.

No smiles.

No games with other children.

And when you're old enough to get married.

No man'll have you.

Not because of you, loves, you're beautiful children, you'll be beautiful women.

And clever and . . .

But who could have you knowing how you were made.

This is what I've given you.

Children.

A lifeless life. Dried and barren. Lived in shadow.

Creon.

You're the only father they have now.

I'm nothing.

Don't let them beg, don't abandon them.

They're your blood too.

Be kind to them.

They feel so helpless in my arms.

I can't protect them.

Promise me Creon.

Touch my hand.

He reaches out to CREON. CREON draws back.

OEDIPUS: Loves.

If you were old enough to understand, I'd tell you what has happened to you.

But for now.
I can only give you this advice.
Live.
Live anyway.
Live.
And I hope your life is happier than mine.

CREON: That's enough.
Take him inside.

OEDIPUS: Let me hold them a minute more.
Just a minute.

CREON: Leave the children now.

OEDIPUS: I'll let them go Creon but on one condition.

CREON: What?

OEDIPUS: You drive me to the mountains.

CREON: If you want.

OEDIPUS: You promise me?

CREON: I said. I'll do it.

OEDIPUS: Then take me now.

CREON: Let go of the children –

The CHILDREN are taken from OEDIPUS. The GUARDS avoid touching OEDIPUS but handle the CHILDREN instead.

OEDIPUS: No – No.
You savages let them go.
No don't take them.
No.
I order you.
No.

CREON: Still boss?

Still master?
Boss of what?
Horror.

All leave apart from OEDIPUS and the CHORUS. OEDIPUS in utter abjection. Kneeling. He crawls towards the pool.

CHORUS: Look at him.
This Is Oedipus.
Dam builder.
Road make.
Law maker.
Visionary.
He was been consumed by the fire of his own life.
And is now ashes.
We see him and feel nothing.
Look at him closely.
What do you see.
Nothing beyond.
Only ashes.
And the memory of the fire.

End

Other plays published by Capercaillie Books

Blooded by Isabel Wright
ISBN 0-9549625-4-0

Electra by Tom McGrath
ISBN 0-9549625-2-4

Opium Eater by Andrew Dallmeyer
ISBN 0-9549625-3-2

The Salt Wound by Stephen Greenhorn
ISBN 0-9549625-0-8

Dissent by Stephen Greenhorn
ISBN 0-9545206-9-6

£8.99

Available from Booksource
Tel: +44(0)8702 402 182 Fax: +44(0) 1415 570 189
email: customerservices@booksource.net

Web orders at www.capercailliebooks.co.uk

Made in the USA
Columbia, SC
14 August 2018